Gina Rees

For Puddles,
my angel.
Thank you for sharing your
special place with us.

Published by Forward Press

Printed by Solent Design Studio

ISBN 978-1-915237-29-3

Copyright © 2023 Gina Rees

MY SPECIAL PLACE

written and illustrated

by

Gina Rees

There's a special place I know, a magical place full of wonder and surprise.

It's a secret place though, hidden away for most of the year.

I can take you there, but first you must be very, very patient...

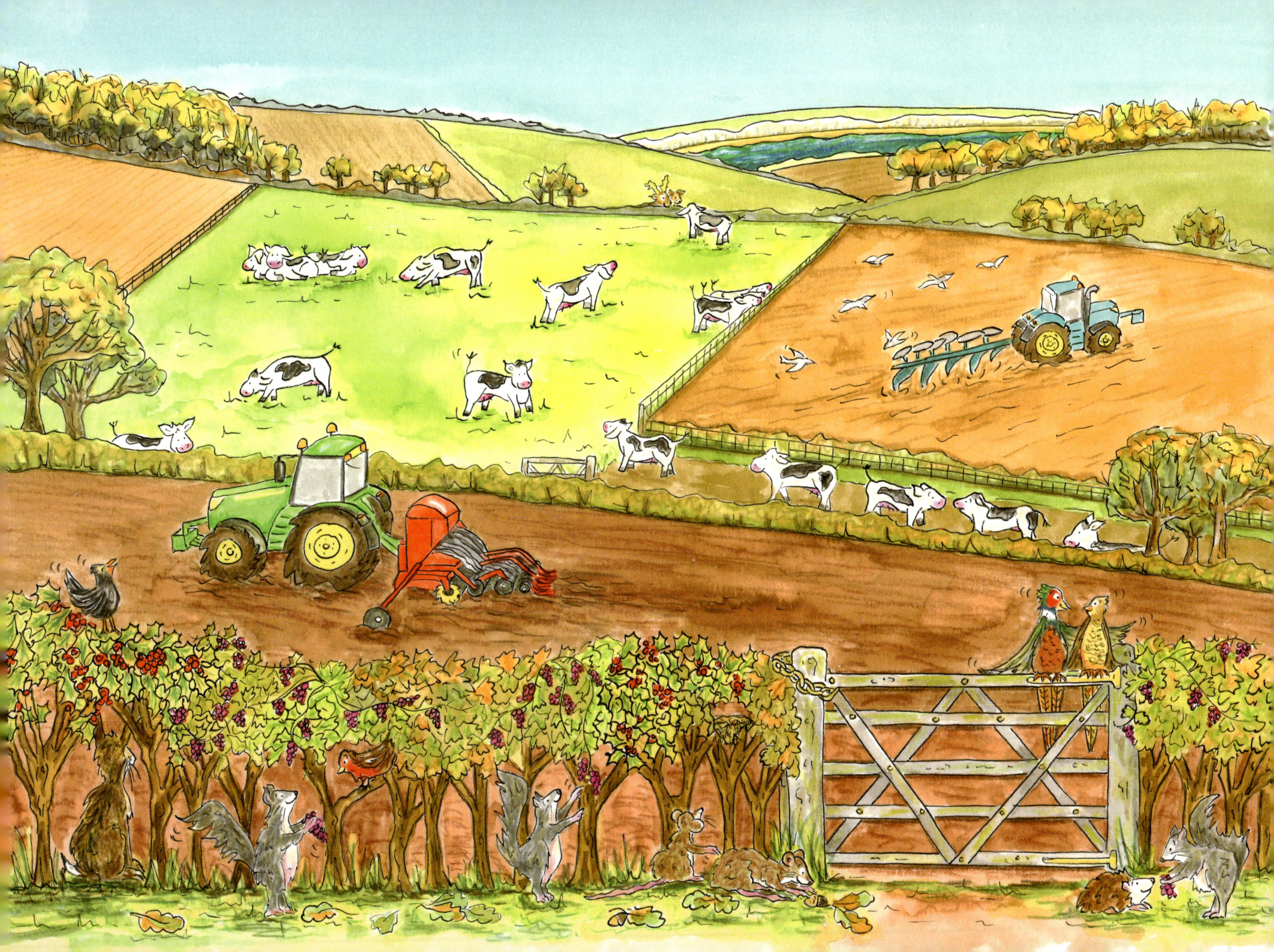

Patient through the dark misty days and the long cold nights.

Patient through the crisp and crunchy frosty mornings.

Patient as you wait, wait for this wondrous place to rest, repair and recharge.

Then as the rain starts to fall

and the sun begins to shine,

the magic begins to stir.

Slowly, wonderful things start to happen.

And when it's ready, a little glimmer of green appears, a little glimmer of hope.

Hope that this enchanting place is starting to wake up!

Soon the glimmer of green begins to swell and sway in the warm, gentle breeze.

Day by day,

week by week,

month by month,

it gets bigger and stronger.

Just like

the hidden special place

that magically ripples through,

and snuggles within, this flourishing field.

Then one day, the green ripens into a golden swell and the magic cannot be hidden or contained any more.

Suddenly a beautiful ocean wondrously appears.

Just like that, this special place has woken up and, at long last, is ready to be explored.

It's fun to play on the shore for a while.

There are so many treasures to see and find.

You can even dip your toes in, if you are feeling brave.

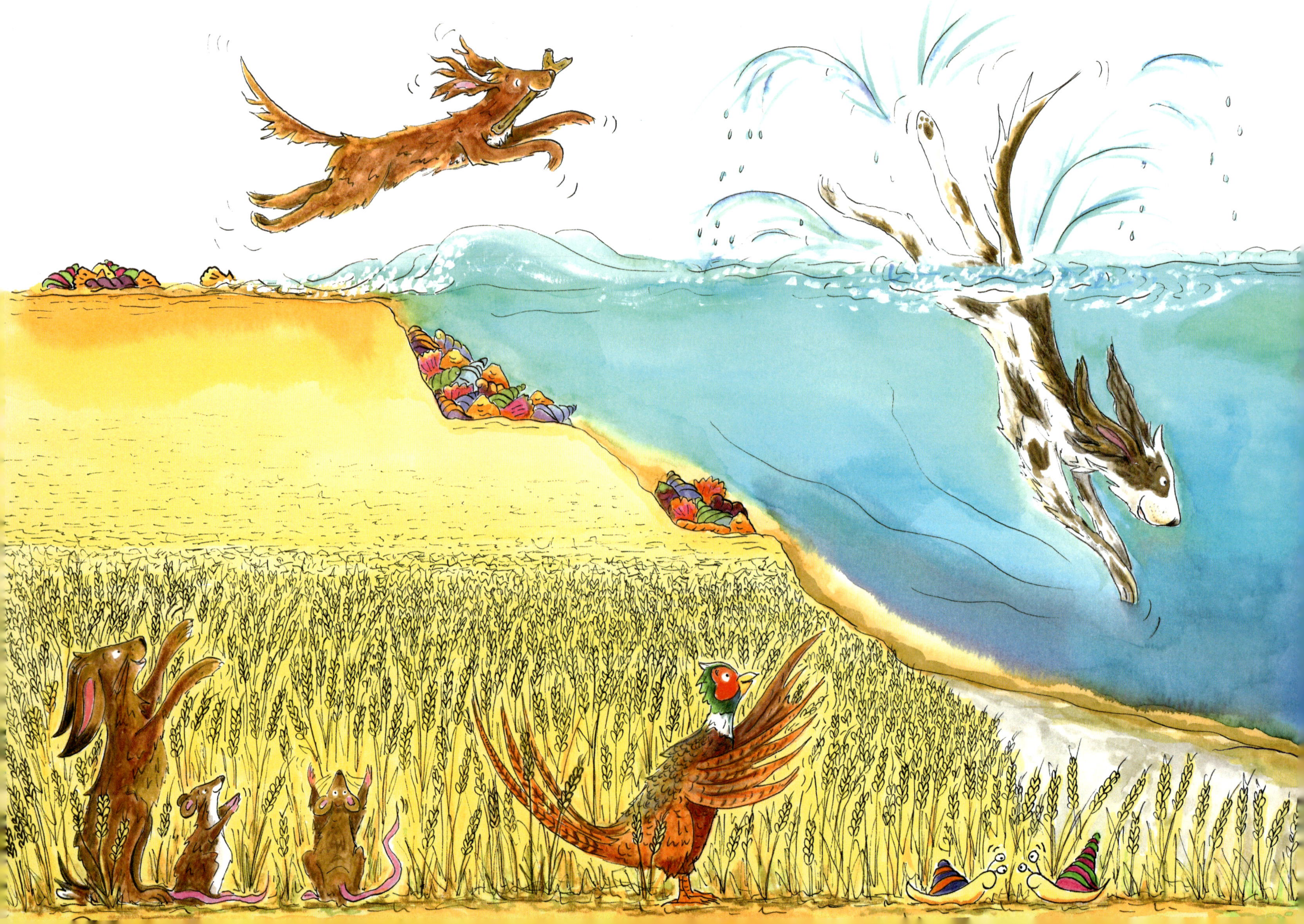

But the real adventures and

best treasures are to be found

INSIDE...

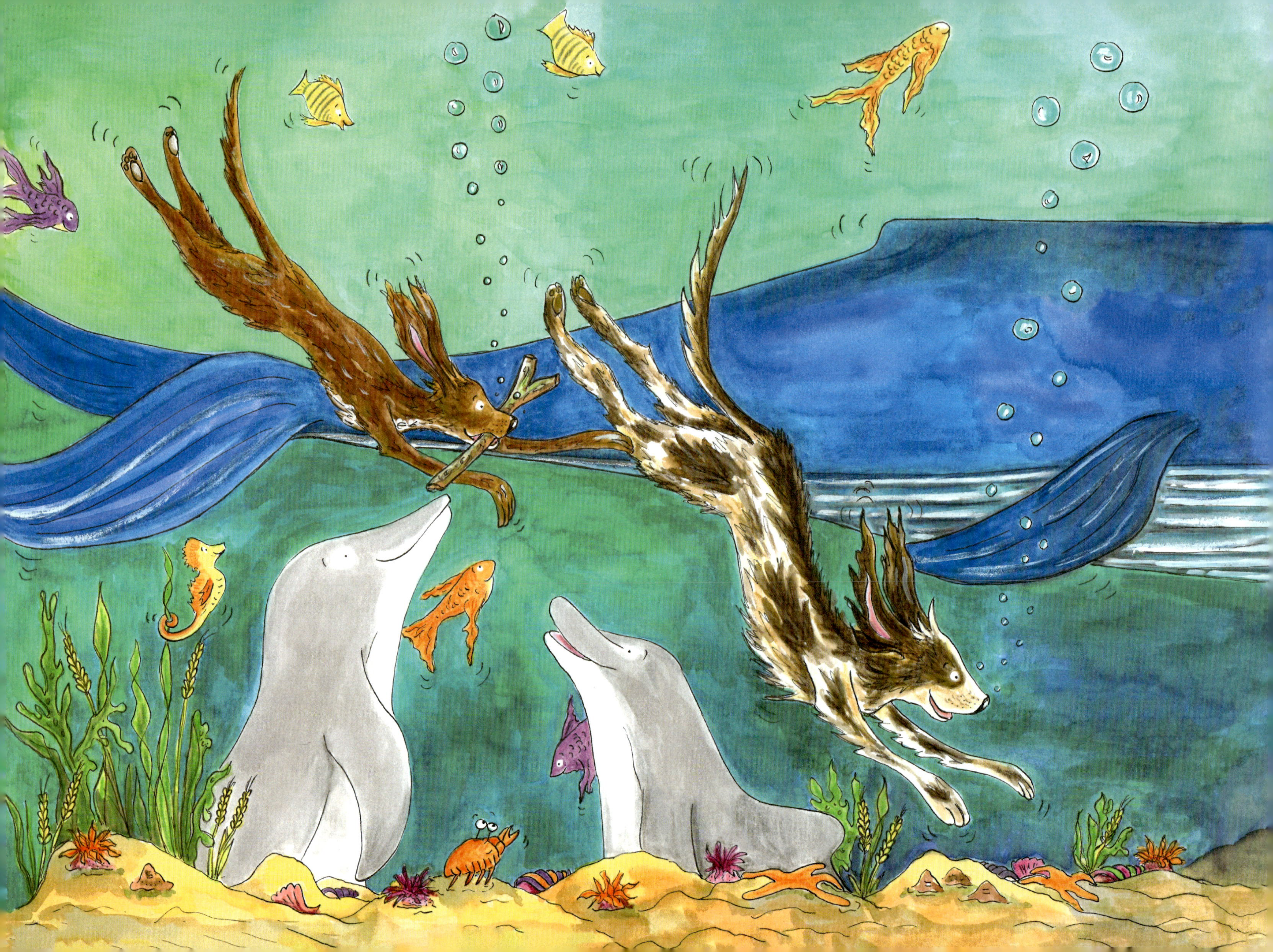

Deep into this secret and hidden, underwater world.

There are creatures to meet and new experiences to be had.

So much to do, but sadly not enough time.

As the golden swell withers and bakes in the hot sun, this wonderful, watery playground starts to fade and disappear.

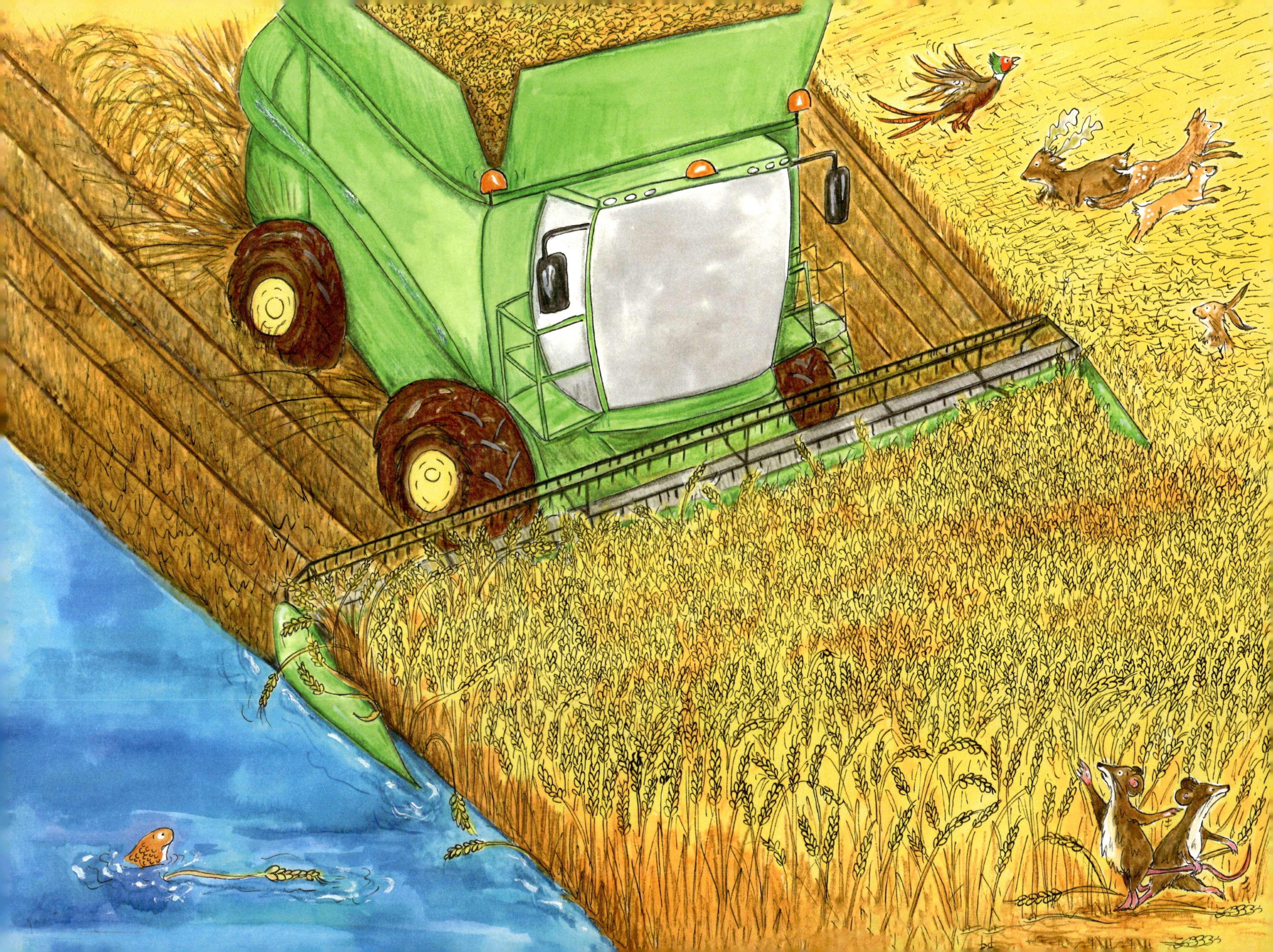

Slowly,

slowly,

bit by bit,

it ebbs away,

until, just

like that,

this special place has GONE!

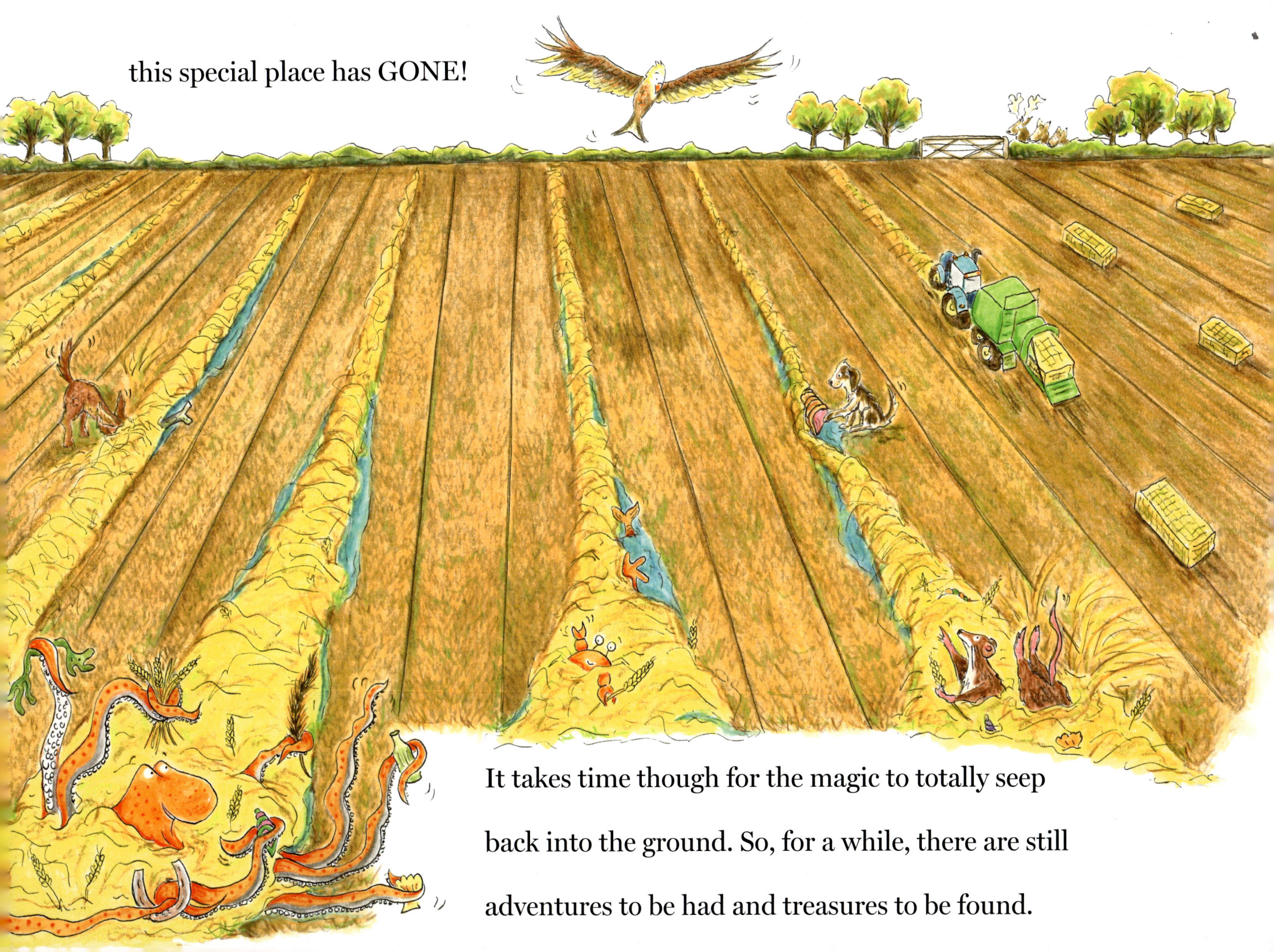

It takes time though for the magic to totally seep back into the ground. So, for a while, there are still adventures to be had and treasures to be found.

Finally, as a rainbow of colours fall all around and onto

what's left of this magical world,

it's time to say goodbye.

Goodbye for now,

but not forever.

This special place just needs time to rest, repair and recharge.

It won't be long before it's ready to share all the amazing hidden adventures and experiences once more.

Until then, you just need to be very, very patient...

Did you see this farm machinery being used?

In which season did you see it?

This is a **tractor** pulling a **plough**. The **plough** is used to turn the soil and get the ground ready to sow the seed.

A **tractor** is used to pull a **seed drill**. The **seed drill** sows the seed straight into the soil.

The seed grows into a crop and a **combine harvester** is used to cut it when it's ready. The **grain cart** collects the grain from the **combine** and takes it away to be stored before it's sold.

This is a **tractor** and **bale grab**. The **tractor** collects the bales of straw and stores them away to use as bedding for the animals.

A **tractor** is used to pull a **baler**. The **baler** squashes the straw that is left and makes it into bales.

This is a **muck spreader**. The **tractor** pulls a tank of manure that it sprays over the soil to help make the seed grow well.

Did you see the crop of **wheat** grow? **Wheat** is used to make flour, which is used to make bread, pasta and cakes and lots of other lovely things.

Spring **Summer** **Autumn** **Winter**